A Sense of Art

Perimeter and Area

Christine Dugan

Consultants

Pamela Dase, M.A.Ed.
National Board Certified Teacher

Barbara Talley, M.S.
Texas A&M University

Publishing Credits

Dona Herweck Rice, *Editor-in-Chief*
Robin Erickson, *Production Director*
Lee Aucoin, *Creative Director*
Timothy J. Bradley, *Illustration Manager*
Sara Johnson, M.S.Ed., *Senior Editor*
Aubrie Nielsen, M.S.Ed., *Associate Education Editor*
Jennifer Kim, M.A.Ed., *Associate Education Editor*
Neri Garcia, *Senior Designer*
Stephanie Reid, *Photo Editor*
Rachelle Cracchiolo, M.S.Ed., *Publisher*

Image Credits

Teacher Created Materials

5301 Oceanus Drive
Huntington Beach, CA 92649-1030
http://www.tcmpub.com

ISBN 978-1-4333-3458-0
© 2012 Teacher Created Materials, Inc.

Table of Contents

Elements of Design

Have you ever painted a room? Have you seen a house being built? It takes a lot of effort to build a place for someone to live or work. Making it look nice on the inside takes hard work, too. You need creativity and imagination for both these jobs.

An architect (AHR-ki-tekt) designs buildings. Being able to imagine how a structure can fill an empty space is an important skill for an architect. An interior designer (in-TEER-ee-er dih-ZAHY-ner) decides how to use the space inside a building. People in these jobs rely on a sense of art to make buildings look nice both outside and inside.

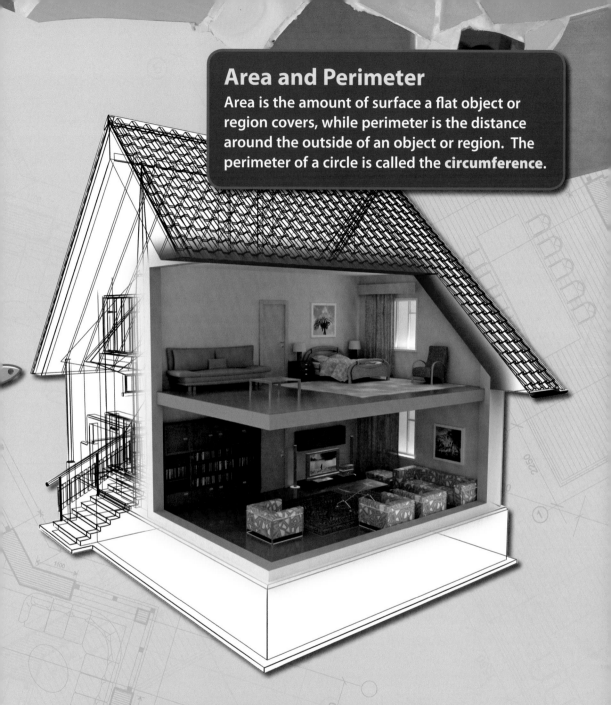

Area and Perimeter

Area is the amount of surface a flat object or region covers, while perimeter is the distance around the outside of an object or region. The perimeter of a circle is called the **circumference**.

How do people in design jobs use math skills? Knowing about shapes and how they fit together is essential (uh-SEN-shuhl) for building a new home. Also, understanding **area** and **perimeter** (puh-RIM-i-ter) helps them plan how to use a space and measure its **dimensions** (dih-MEN-shuhns).

Most rooms in a house or other large building are shaped like a square or rectangle. However, not all spaces are like this. Rooms can come in all shapes and sizes.

This castle in Italy was built and rebuilt over many years. Some rooms in this castle have been added to the rest of the structure. Some of the spaces in the castle are **polygons**. One room is even a **trapezoid**!

Conversano Castle, Italy

The Pentagon

The Pentagon is the building where the United States Department of Defense is housed in Washington, D.C. It is shaped like a pentagon.

Trapezoids

The **formula** for the area of a trapezoid is $A = \frac{1}{2}(b_1 + b_2) h$. Notice that b_1 and b_2 are the parallel sides and are called the bases of the trapezoid. The height, h, describes how tall the trapezoid is. The height may not be a side of the trapezoid.

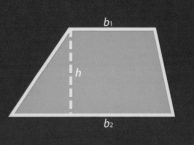

Architects and interior designers have to work with spaces that have different shapes all the time. It can make a job more challenging or more interesting.

LET'S EXPLORE MATH

A designer needs to know how much baseboard to purchase for a room that is shaped like a trapezoid. Remember that the perimeter of a polygon is the sum of the lengths of its sides. Find the perimeter of the room below.

The designer also needs to know the area of this room in order to purchase carpet for the floor. Use the formula for the area of a trapezoid to find the area of the room.

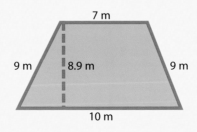

Designing the interior of a new space is a big job. It means working with a blank space and deciding what looks best. It also means knowing how to make the room useful. Design work includes planning the structure of the space and picking materials for the walls and the floor. Furniture and artwork are added to make the space attractive, usable, and comfortable.

Measurement is very important in design work. Architects need to know exactly how large spaces are within a building. They have to measure the exact length, width, and height of all the rooms. These rooms must fit together in a way that makes sense.

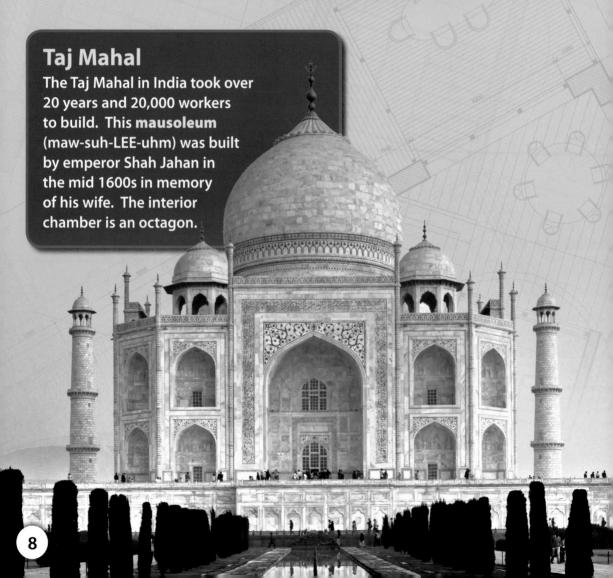

Taj Mahal

The Taj Mahal in India took over 20 years and 20,000 workers to build. This **mausoleum** (maw-suh-LEE-uhm) was built by emperor Shah Jahan in the mid 1600s in memory of his wife. The interior chamber is an octagon.

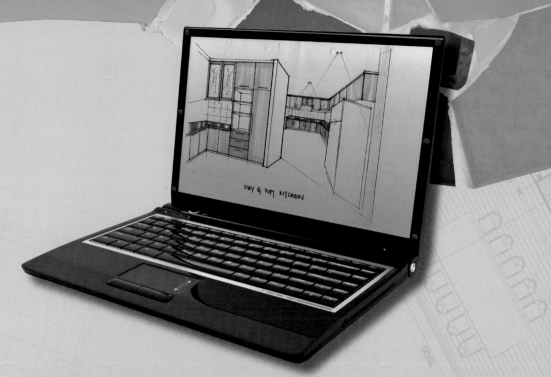

Interior designers also have to measure spaces. They use these measurements to design and decorate rooms. Designers decide where cabinets will fit in a new kitchen. They have to know how much carpet or paint is needed for a room. They also have to make decisions about the size and amount of furniture based on the shape and size of the room.

LET'S EXPLORE MATH

A regular polygon has sides that are all the same length.

Find the perimeter of this regular octagon.

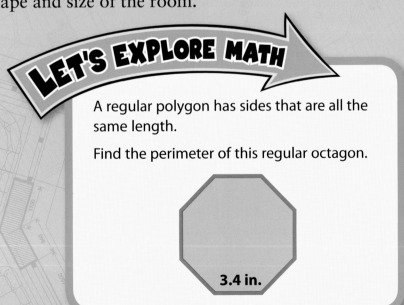

3.4 in.

Observing Circles in Design

There are many different shapes in architecture and interior design. Many architects and designers include circles in a building or room design. Circles are one way to make a room or an object look **unique**. A round room or a round skylight is a way to use circles in buildings.

gazebo

Pi

Pi (PAHY) is a constant in math whose value is the ratio of the circumference of any circle to the diameter. Since pi is an **irrational number**, it cannot be expressed exactly as a fraction or decimal. Mathematicians use the approximations $\frac{22}{7}$ and 3.14 for pi.

LET'S EXPLORE MATH

Look at the formulas below for the area and circumference of a circle. The *d* represents the **diameter** and the *r* represents the **radius**.

3.1 in.

Circumference of a circle: $C = \pi d$ or $C = 2\pi r$

Area of a circle: $A = \pi r^2$

Use $\frac{22}{7}$ or 3.14 for π.

Emily is making a model of a park. The circle above is the base of her model **gazebo**. What is the circumference of this circle? What is the area of this circle? Round your answers to the nearest hundredth.

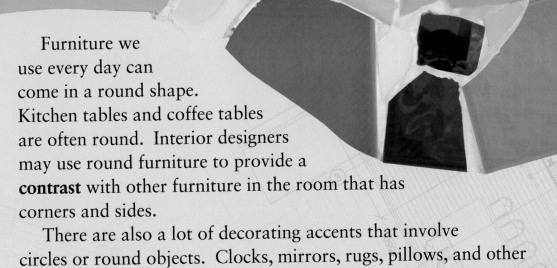

Furniture we use every day can come in a round shape. Kitchen tables and coffee tables are often round. Interior designers may use round furniture to provide a **contrast** with other furniture in the room that has corners and sides.

There are also a lot of decorating accents that involve circles or round objects. Clocks, mirrors, rugs, pillows, and other decorative items may be round as well.

dome at St. Peter's Basilica, Italy

Temple of Heaven, China

Triangles in Design

Triangles are another useful shape in architecture and design. Architects want to make strong structures. This is why using triangles is smart engineering. Builders have used triangles for centuries. They provide stable support in construction. Think of the famous Egyptian pyramids. These strong structures have stood for over 4,000 years!

Many of our buildings and bridges today include triangles in their design. Look closely at the bridge below. The arch of the bridge is designed to include overlapping triangles. This use of triangles makes a strong bridge. It is also interesting to look at!

the Pyramids at Giza, Eygpt

Humber Bay Arch Bridge, Canada

Another famous example of triangles in design is at the Louvre (LOO-vruh) Museum. This pyramid-shaped building in Paris, France, includes many triangles. Its modern construction stands out from the older, more traditional buildings around it.

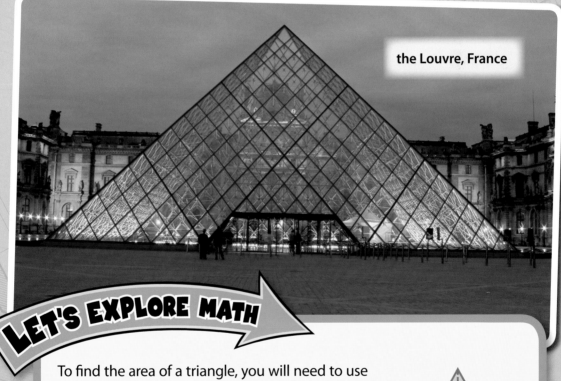

the Louvre, France

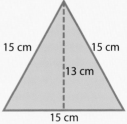

LET'S EXPLORE MATH

To find the area of a triangle, you will need to use the formula $A = \frac{1}{2}(bh)$. The height (h) of the triangle describes how tall the triangle is. The height is always **perpendicular** (pur-puhn-DIK-yuh-ler) to the base (b).

15 cm 15 cm

13 cm

15 cm

a. Find the perimeter of the triangle.

b. Find the area of the triangle.

An Architect at Work

All good design ideas must start with a plan. Architects and designers have to plan their ideas using special drawings. These are called **blueprints**. The blueprints are used to show others what a finished building or interior will look like.

In these drawings, different shapes are used to show various parts of a building or a room. These shapes represent objects like doors, counters, fireplaces, or windows. The designers must draw everything to **scale**. This means all parts of the drawing are shown in relation to the size of actual objects.

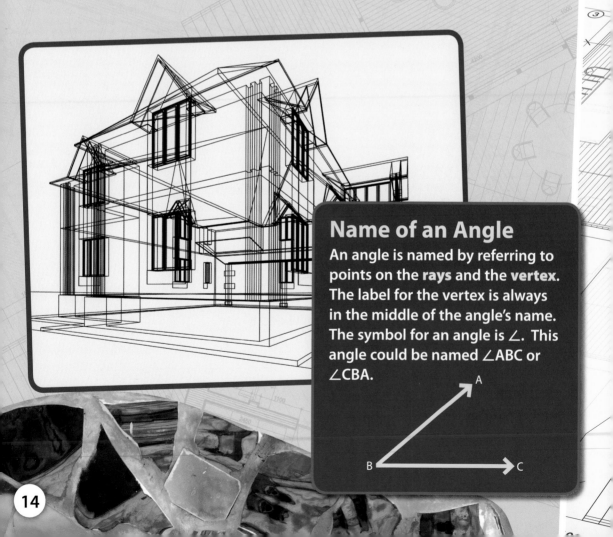

Name of an Angle

An angle is named by referring to points on the **rays** and the **vertex**. The label for the vertex is always in the middle of the angle's name. The symbol for an angle is ∠. This angle could be named ∠ABC or ∠CBA.

Look at the blueprint below. The designer included shapes to show the final layout when construction is finished. This blueprint also includes **angles** that are drawn very carefully.

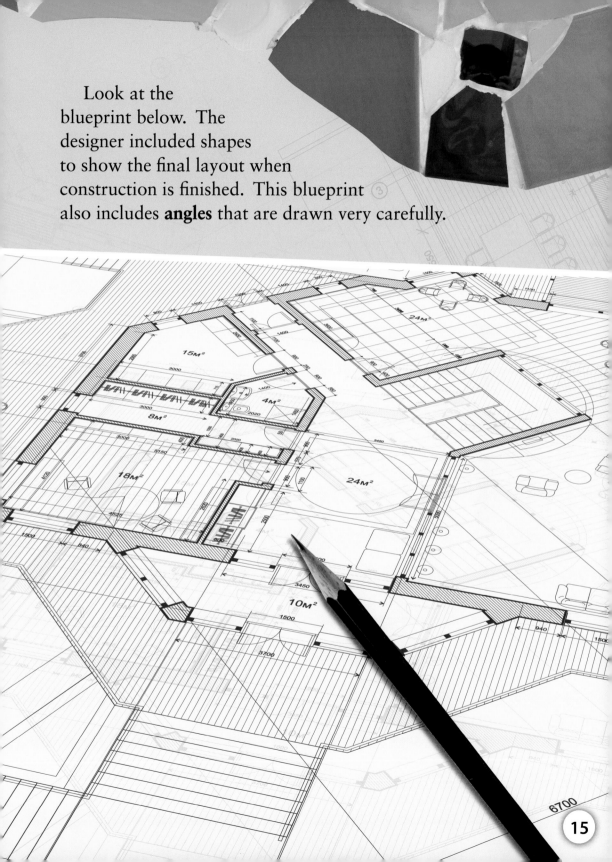

Measuring Angles

Designers want to make their drawings as precise as possible. They have to pay attention to the details in their drawings. Shapes and lines need to be extremely accurate. They measure angles to make sure the drawing represents the size and shape of the new building.

A **protractor** (proh-TRAK-ter) is one tool that is used to measure an angle. Different shapes have different angle measurements.

Designers use angles to plan walls, windows, doorways, and other parts of a building.

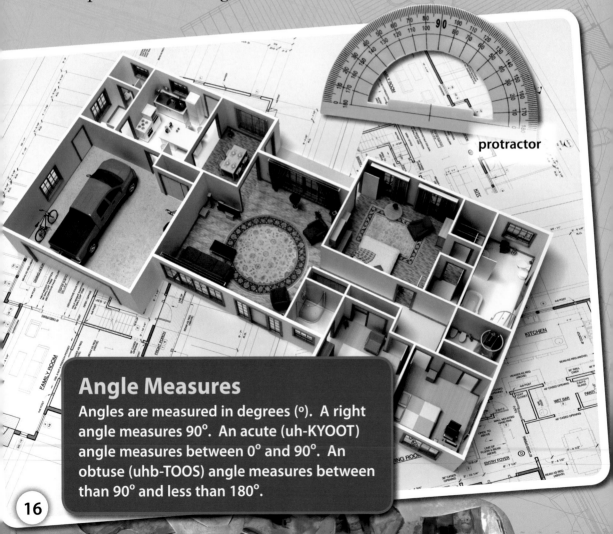

protractor

Angle Measures

Angles are measured in degrees (°). A right angle measures 90°. An acute (uh-KYOOT) angle measures between 0° and 90°. An obtuse (uhb-TOOS) angle measures between than 90° and less than 180°.

Hearst Tower, New York

Triangles and Quadrilaterals

A triangle has three vertices. That means it has three angles. The sum of the angles inside a triangle is always 180°.

A quadrilateral has four vertices and four angles. The sum of the angles inside a quadrilateral is always 360°.

Using CAD and BIM Software

Architects want precise blueprints. They use computer-aided design (CAD) software to help them get the precision (pri-SIZH-uhn) they need. This type of software helps architects and people who work in construction. They can create technical drawings that are easily shared and viewed by others. This allows different people to contribute to the plans of a building.

Building information modeling (BIM) is an advanced form of CAD software. BIM allows architects to design buildings in three dimensions.

This designer is using 3-D CAD software. The glasses she is wearing make the images on the touch screen appear in three dimensions.

Architects can use BIM to show others what a building will look like after construction is complete. It makes a realistic image of a finished building. BIM also helps builders and designers plan ahead for materials and labor. BIM allows architects to provide detailed information about a building—down to the number of nails needed for its construction!

LET'S EXPLORE MATH

You can find the area of an irregular polygon by dividing it into regular polygons. Look at the quadrilateral below. Divide it into a triangle and a trapezoid and find their areas. Then find the area of the whole figure.

a. What is the area of the triangle?

b. What is the area of the trapezoid?

c. Find the sum of the two areas to determine the area of the quadrilateral.

19 cm
25 cm
16 cm
32 cm

CAD in Fashion Design

Architects aren't the only professionals who use CAD software. Many fashion designers also use CAD to create their designs. This allows them to work quicker and waste less material while creating their designs.

Design Tools

CAD software is essential for design work. Yet architects and designers cannot rely entirely on a computer to create drafts and pictures of their work. They still need to be able to sketch ideas. In order to do so, they have to use other tools to put their ideas on paper.

Architects use special paper for their designs. Architects may use graph paper that has both horizontal and vertical lines. This helps them organize their drawings and sketch objects to scale.

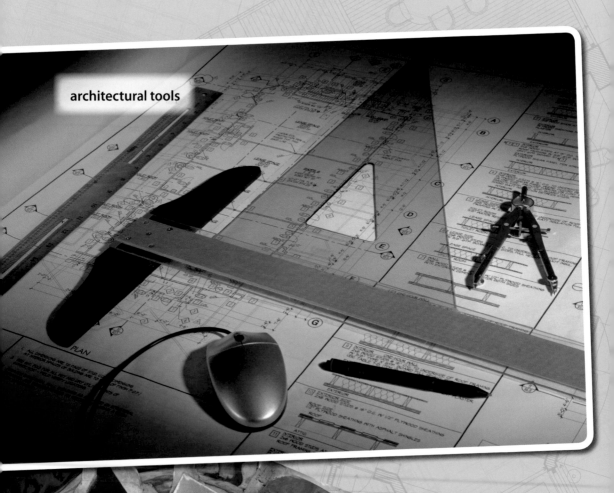

architectural tools

A T-square is another helpful tool. It is a drawing tool used as a guide for drawing straight lines. Some architects may also use a triangle ruler to help them draw lines and measure angles.

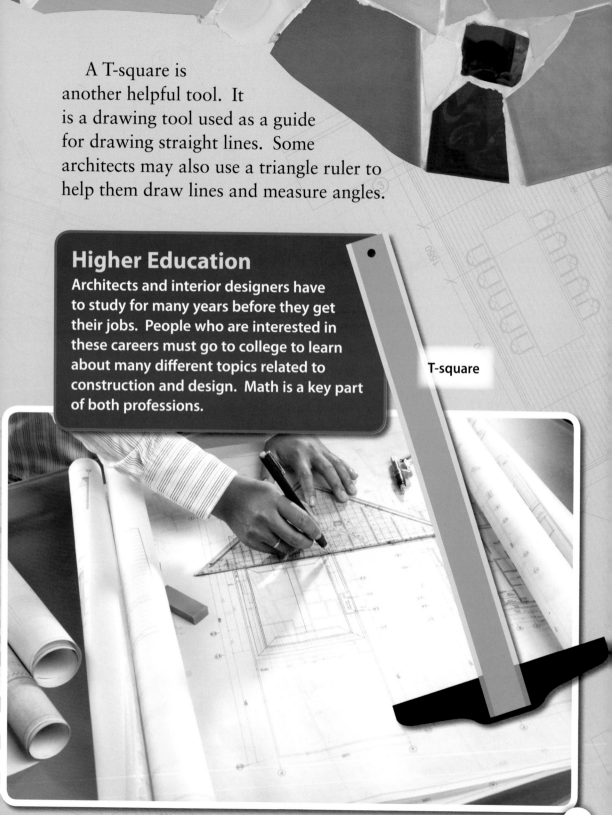

Higher Education

Architects and interior designers have to study for many years before they get their jobs. People who are interested in these careers must go to college to learn about many different topics related to construction and design. Math is a key part of both professions.

T-square

Mosaics in Design

Mosaics (moh-ZEY-ikz) are an important part of design. A mosaic is a picture or design made with small pieces of glass, tile, stone, or other material. A mosaic may have pieces that are different colors, sizes, or shapes. An artist is able to arrange the small pieces in a way that is interesting and unique.

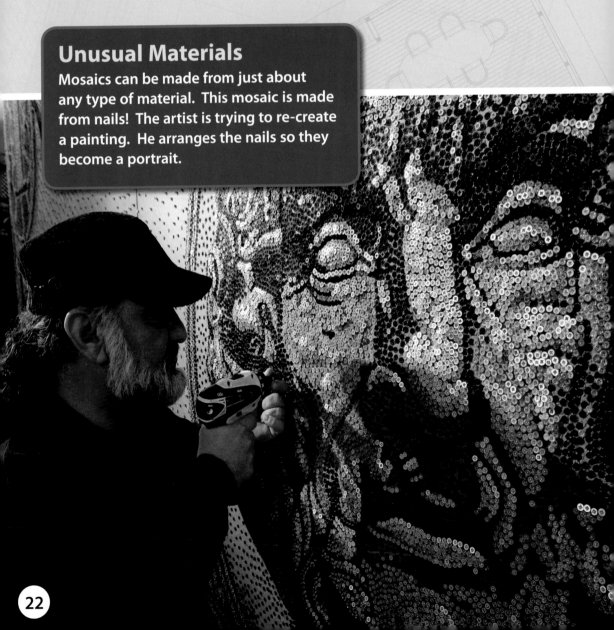

Unusual Materials

Mosaics can be made from just about any type of material. This mosaic is made from nails! The artist is trying to re-create a painting. He arranges the nails so they become a portrait.

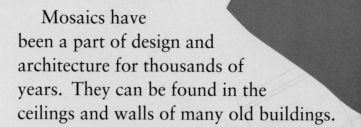

Mosaics have been a part of design and architecture for thousands of years. They can be found in the ceilings and walls of many old buildings.

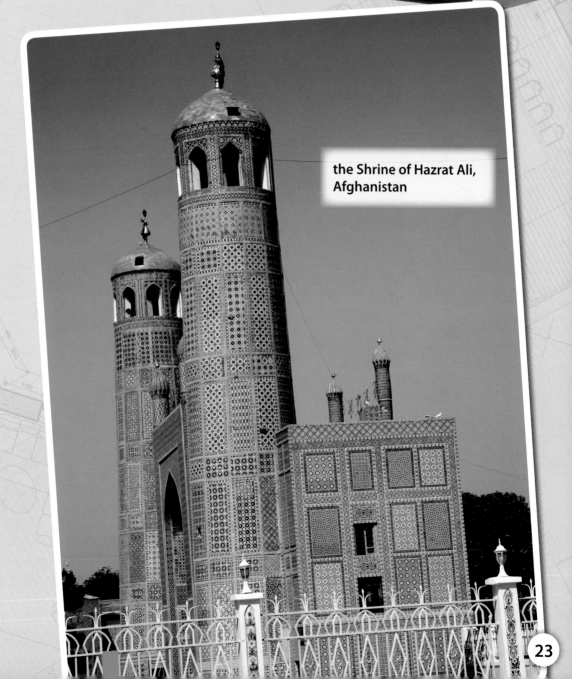

the Shrine of Hazrat Ali, Afghanistan

Mosaics can be found in just about every corner of the world. You can find mosaics in ancient temples and cathedrals. Or you can spot mosaics in backyards, parks, schools, and even inside homes.

Antoni Gaudí (an-TUH-nee gow-DEE) was an architect in the late 19th century. His unique style can be seen in buildings all over Barcelona, Spain. Gaudí covered many of his designs in colorful tile mosaics. Park Güell (GWEY) is one of the best examples of Gaudí's curved stone structures, sculptures, and mosaics.

Park Güell, Spain

In Tehran (te-RAN), Iran, visitors can see unique architecture as well. The Golestan Palace is almost 500 years old. It includes mosaics on the walls, ceilings, and walkways. This style of artwork adds to the history and beauty of this old building.

Golestan Palace, Iran

LET'S EXPLORE MATH

Look at the drawing of the mosaic design below.

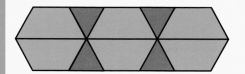

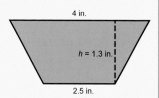

h = 1.3 in.

1.5 in.

4 in.

h = 1.3 in.

2.5 in.

a. The red stone is an equilateral triangle. What is its perimeter?

b. What is the area of the triangular stone? Round your answer to the nearest hundredth.

c. The perimeter of the trapezoidal stone is 9.5 in. What are the lengths of the unlabeled sides?

d. Find the area of the trapezoidal stone. Round your answer to the nearest hundredth.

The Art of Building

Building a new structure requires more than just nails and wood. Architects and interior designers use a lot of different skills to plan and construct amazing new buildings. They must understand how to use space in ways that make the most sense. They have to use math skills to measure and estimate. They also need to understand perimeter and area to be precise and accurate.

There is one other skill that is essential, too. The people who work in these professions must have good instincts about what works. They must understand how people live and work. They have to know how important a living or work space is in our daily lives.

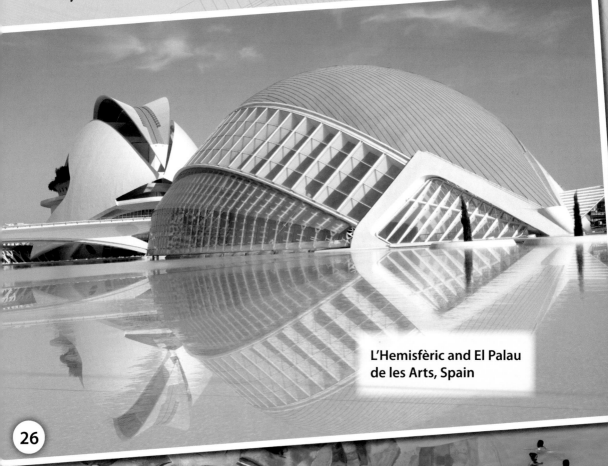

L'Hemisfèric and El Palau de les Arts, Spain

Think about this the next time you are sitting in your own home or at school. Consider what you might do differently if you could build a home, school, or office building. How would you use a sense of art to design your dream space?

Burj al Arab Hotel, Dubai

Vatican Museum, Italy

Building a Tree House

Jeff and Maria are working on a big project in their backyard. They are building a tree house with their father. Their father has helped them sketch a design to show how they want the finished product to look.

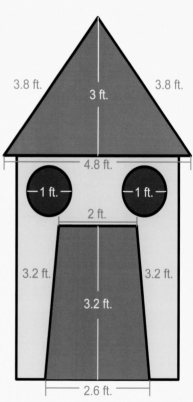

Solve It!

a. Find the perimeter and area of the door, the front of the roof, and each window of the tree house. Round your answers to the nearest hundredth.

b. What other measurements would be helpful for Jeff and Maria to know before they start building? Why?

Use the steps below to help you find the solutions.

Step 1: Find the perimeter and area of the door. Add all the sides together to find the perimeter. Use the formula for the area of a trapezoid: $A = \frac{1}{2}(b_1 + b_2)h$.

Step 2: Find the perimeter and area of the roof. Add all the sides together to find the perimeter. Use the formula for the area of a triangle: $A = \frac{1}{2}bh$.

Step 3: Find the circumference and area of one window. Use the formula for the circumference of a circle: $C = \pi d$ or $C = 2\pi r$. Use the formula for the area of a circle: $A = \pi r^2$.

Glossary

angles—figures formed by two rays that share an endpoint

area—the surface a flat object or region covers, measured in square units

blueprints—special drawings created by architects and designers to provide a model of how a finished building or interior will look

circumference—the distance around a circle

contrast—a difference, as compared with something else

diameter—the distance across a circle through the center

dimensions—measurements of the size of an object, such as length, width, height, and depth

formula—a general mathematical rule represented in symbols, numbers, or letters, often in the form of an equation

gazebo—a circular building that is slightly elevated and usually found in parks or outdoor places

irrational number—a number that cannot be expressed exactly as a ratio of two integers

mausoleum—a large or fancy tomb

mosaics—pictures or designs made with small pieces of material

perimeter—the distance around the outside of an object or region

perpendicular—forming a right angle

polygons—two-dimensional shapes with three or more straight sides

protractor—an instrument used to measure and draw angles

radius—the distance from the center of a circle to any point on the circle

rays—parts of lines that begin at a point and extend indefinitely in one direction from the starting point

scale—a ratio representing the size of an illustration or reproduction in relation to the object it represents

trapezoid—a polygon that has exactly one pair of parallel sides, called bases

unique—being the only one of its kind

vertex—a point at which two rays, lines, or line segments meet to form an angle

Index

Let's Explore Math

Page 7:

perimeter: 35 m

area: 75.65 m^2

Page 9:

27.2 in.

Page 10:

circumference: 19.47 in.

area: 30.18 in.^{2}

Page 13:

perimeter: 45 cm

area: 97.5 cm^2

Page 19:

a. 237.5 cm^2

b. 456 cm^2

c. 693.5 cm^2

Page 25:

a. 4.5 in.

b. 0.98 in.^{2}

c. 1.5 in.

d. 4.23 in.^{2}

Problem-Solving Activity

a. door—perimeter: 11 ft., area: 7.36 ft.^{2}; roof—perimeter: 12.4 ft., area: 7.2 ft.^{2}; window—circumference: 3.14 ft., area: 0.79 ft.^{2}

b. Answers will vary, but may include the height of the tree house from the ground (since they will need to build steps to get up to it), the dimensions of the floor (for buying materials), or how high the windows will be from the floor and how far they will be from the vertices (to know exactly where to cut the openings for them).